Lisa Shively

Fat Little Crockin' Cookbook

Let's Get Crockin'!

Printed in the U.S.A. by
Lisa Shively Cookbooks
P.O. Box 2123
Eden, N.C. 27289
www.fromourhometoyours.net

ISBN-13: 978-0-9766756-3-1
ISBN-10: 0-9766756-3-3
LCCN- 2006906830

A Note from Lisa

"Lisa, why a crockin' cookbook?" Well, I'll tell you! There is nothing nicer than coming home from a long day to have dinner hot and ready to serve. For those of us who can't afford to have our own live-in cook, this is as close to living that life as we will probably ever get.

So many times I am told "I just don't have time to cook". This is my way of saying, “Yes, you do and here's how to do it.” Using this book will give you more time to slow down and enjoy those around you and isn't that what life should really be about?

Anytime I can throw something in a pot, turn it on, walk away, come back later and have dinner ready…
honey, that' my kind of cooking!

While writing this book, I have found that when it comes to crock cooking, there are several kinds of people. There are the ones who love their crocks and use them all the time. There are those who just never "got into" crock cooking. And there are those who used theirs often when they first got one, but over the years, they would end up in a closet and eventually at a yard sale or a thrift store. This book is for everyone, no matter which group you fall into.

If you are in the market for a new crock cooker remember, it doesn't have to be fancy. They do make some with bonus features that are nice, but not necessary. I use the standard sized 3-1/2 to 4 quart crock cooker and that is what all of these recipes were tested in.

This collection of recipes will make you glad that you're a crock owner and user. Even I have been amazed at the recipes that I came across when I started to work on this book. If you have read my other books, then you know I have always believed in crock cooking because I have a good many recipes for them in my other books.

This book is 100 of my new favorites and I do believe that you will love them, too.

So sit back, read, enjoy and make a grocery list. Easy meals and desserts are in your future.

Happy Crockin'

Lisa

Tips for using this book

* All of these recipes were tested in a standard 3-1/2 to 4 quart crock cooker. If you have a different size, you will need to adjust the cooking times. (A larger pot would take a little less time.)

* If you are cooking meats that have been cut through a bone, especially pork chops or ribs, be sure to rinse the meat well to remove any remaining "bone dust".

* If a recipe calls for “flour”, use “all-purpose flour”.

* While cooking, do not open your pot unless the directions say to. For each time the lid is opened, you will need to add 15 minutes to the cooking time. It takes that long to return to the correct cooking temperature.

* If a recipe calls for butter, margarine can be used. (I almost always use margarine.)

* If a recipe says to use a "greased" crock, spray with non-stick cooking spray before adding ingredients to the pot.

* Do not pre-heat your crock before adding food to it. The recipes are tested with a crock beginning at room temperature.

* Some recipes require you to brown meat before adding it to your crock. While crocks do completely cook the meat, they don't brown the meat.

Holiday Suggestions

January-New Year's Day

Money in Your Pockets

Collard Greens

Eating greens on New Year's Day is a tradition that is supposed to bring you a year of financial wealth.

2 bunches of collard greens, chopped
1 lb. ham hock or meaty ham bone
2-4 T. sliced jalapenos from a jar
1 tsp. vegetable oil
salt and pepper to taste
2 c. water

Chop greens and place into a large pot. Fill pot half full with water. Cook until wilted (so they will fit into crock). Rinse greens and layer into your crock with ham hocks and jalapenos. Add oil, salt and pepper to taste and water. Cover and cook on high for 1 hour then reduce heat and cook on low for 8-10 hours.

I'm not very good at washing fresh greens; that's why I wilt them first in water. Drain off the dirty water and rinse several times before adding them to your crock.

<u>February-Valentine's Day</u>

Sweetheart's Fudge Fondue

Warning: I can not be held responsible for the actions you may take after tasting this fondue. Be prepared for romance to follow shortly after serving.

2 c. semisweet chocolate chips
1 can Eagle's Brand condensed milk
1 (7oz.) marshmallow creme
½ c. milk
1 tsp. vanilla

Combine all ingredients in your crock. Cover and cook on low for 1 hour. Stir until smooth before serving.

Serve with toothpicks or fondue forks with pineapple or banana chunks, apple slices, marshmallows or cubed pound cake.... a real party pleaser! If you are serving a romantic treat for the two of you, serve in a pretty little bowl or custard cup.

March-Race Parties

Rubber Burnin' Race Day Dip

I know that race days occur at other times of the year, but this dip celebrates the Indy 500 held in March. Even if you don't follow racing...you will love this dip!

1 (16 oz.) jar hot salsa
1 (15oz.) can chili with beans
1 (8 oz.) bag cubed cheddar cheese

Combine all ingredients into your crock. Cover and cook on low for 2 hours. Stir well before serving. Serve with Doritos. For a big or extremely hungry crowd make a double batch.

If this doesn't get your motor running,
honey, nothing will!
This stuff is hot!

April-Easter

Bunny Hoppin' Coconut "Pie"

This pie will get all your bunnies hoppin'.

2 c. milk
¼ c. butter
1-½ tsp. vanilla
4 eggs
1 ½ c. flaked or shredded coconut
1 c. sugar
½ c. Bisquick

Place all ingredients into a blender. Process until smooth. Pour into your crock. Cover and cook on low for 6-8 hours or until set. Allow to cool, then place crock into the refrigerator.

This is a creamy, custard-like pie that is best served cold. It really does slice like a "real" pie. When my husband wants coconut pie, this is the one he wants.

May-Mother's Day

Mama's Chicken Cordon Bleu

Remember- Mama shouldn't have to cook on Mother's Day, but if she has to, she won't mind if it's this easy and good. But y'all bring the other stuff...and presents.

4-6 boneless chicken breasts
4-6 slices Swiss or Mozzarella cheese
4-6 slices of deli ham
1 can cream of chicken or celery soup
$\frac{1}{4}$ c. milk

Wrap each chicken breast with a slice of cheese, then a slice of ham. Secure with a toothpick and place into your crock. In a bowl, combine soup with milk and pour over chicken. Cover and cook on low for 4 hours. Serve over noodles or dressing.

For a special meal, cook the "Corn Stuffing Balls" with "Chicken Cordon Bleu" placed on top of dressing. The cook time is the same. This is so easy and delicious. It's just plain naughty!

June- Father's Day

Big Dave's Mesquite Beef

Now the same rules don't apply to Father's Day...they weren't really thinking they'd have to cook anyway. This is so good and easy - it will make everybody happy!

1 (3lb.) chuck roast
1 c. Lawry's Mesquite Marinade
with Lime Juice, divided

Place roast into your crock. Pour $\frac{3}{4}$ cup of marinade over roast. Cover and cook on low for 8-10 hours. Remove meat from crock and pour liquid into a bowl. (You'll want to dip into it.) Shred meat and return to pot. Add remaining $\frac{1}{4}$ cup of marinade. Heat thoroughly and serve on rolls, flour tortillas or taco shells.

This is the most incredible use of a chuck roast I have ever had. This is so good; I'd buy the roast even if it wasn't on sale! I named it after my husband because he just loves it. It's absolutely fabulous!

July- Celebrating the 4th

Firecracker Chili Dogs

Well, I don't know where you are, but here it rains <u>every</u> 4th of July...so it's nice not to have to go outside to grill the hot dogs.

1 (1 lb.) pkg. hot dogs
2 (15oz.) cans chili with no beans
½ c. onion, finely chopped
1 (4oz.) can chopped green chilies
1 tsp. chili powder
2 c. shredded cheddar cheese

Place hot dogs into your crock. In a bowl, combine chili, onion, green chilies, and chili powder. Pour over hot dogs. Cover and cook on low for 6-9 hours. Before serving, add cheese and cook until melted. Serve on buns.

Nothing says "Happy 4th of July" more than chili dogs. These are so easy, you will have more time to celebrate!

August-Too Hot for the Oven

Barbeque Chicken

Y'all know what I'm talking about, when it's so hot you don't want to heat the kitchen by cooking in the oven...this is just what you're looking for!

3-4 lbs. chicken pieces
1 medium onion, sliced
1 medium lemon, sliced (optional)
1 (18oz.) barbeque sauce
$\frac{3}{4}$ c. cola, not diet

Place chicken into your crock. Top with onion and lemon slices. In a bowl, combine barbeque sauce and cola. Pour over chicken. Cover and cook on low for 8-10 hours.

I like to use chicken thighs with the skin removed and KC Masterpiece barbeque sauce. Use the sauce that you like best.

September- Labor Day

Take it Easy Spuds 'n Chops

Nobody should have to labor on Labor Day -we all work hard enough. Let's take it easy for this holiday.

1 can cream of mushroom soup
$\frac{1}{4}$ c. water
4 medium potatoes, peeled & cubed
3-5 pork chops, frozen or thawed
pepper to taste

Pour soup and water into your crock and stir well. Add potatoes and pepper to taste. Stir to coat potatoes. Lay pork chops over potatoes. Salt and pepper to taste. Cover and cook on low for 6-8 hours.

This is so good and so easy! No time to thaw those chops? Don't worry. Follow the recipe as directed and they will be perfectly cooked and delicious.

October- Celebrate Fall Harvest

Octoberfest in a Pot

Don't forget to enjoy the fruits of the seasons. When fruits and vegetables are coming in...celebrate them all.

1 lb. Kielbasa or Bratwurst links
5 medium potatoes, peeled & cubed
1 (27 oz.) can sauerkraut
1 apple, chopped
1 small onion, chopped
¼ c. brown sugar
½ tsp. salt

Cut sausage into 1 inch slices. Brown in a skillet on all sides. Rinse sauerkraut and pour into your crock. Add remaining ingredients. Stir in sausages. Cover and cook on high for 4-6 hours or until potatoes are tender.

This is not an everyday "southern" dish, but it is tasty. My husband loves sauerkraut after his travels in Germany and he asks for this often. If you are not a sauerkraut lover, replace it with ½ head of shredded cabbage.

November- Thanksgiving

Turkey & Stuffing

At the end of this meal, you'll feel a bit like a stuffed turkey yourself.

¼ c. onion, chopped
1 stalk celery, sliced
1 (3 lb.) boneless turkey breast roast, thawed and string removed
1 (12oz.) jar turkey gravy
1/3 c. apple juice
1 (6oz.)Stove-Top turkey stuffing mix

Place onion and celery into greased crock. Top with turkey breast roast. Pour jar of gravy and apple juice over turkey. Top with dry stuffing mix. Cover and cook on low for 4-5 hours. A few minutes before serving, turn crock off and remove turkey. Stir stuffing into the onions, celery and juices in pot. Cover and let stand for 10 minutes. Serve stuffing with turkey.

Holidays should not be as stressful as we let them be...slow down and enjoy those around you!

December-Christmas

Holiday Sweet Potato Casserole

This is so good and easy, you won't want to wait for a holiday to serve it. We don't!

2 (29oz.) cans sweet potatoes,drained
1/3 c. butter, melted
2 T. sugar
2 T. brown sugar
1 T. orange juice
2 eggs, beaten
1 c. milk

Drain potatoes and place into a large bowl. Beat potatoes until smooth. Add remaining ingredients, mix well after each addition. Pour into a greased crock. In a bowl, combine topping ingredients until crumbly. Sprinkle over casserole. Cover and cook on low for 6-8 hours.

Topping:

1/3 c. pecans, chopped
1/3 c. brown sugar
2 T. flour
2 tsp. butter

Appetizers & Beverages

(My Little Crockapotamus)

Artichoke Crab Dip

1 (14oz.) can artichoke hearts, drained
1 (8oz.) pkg. cream cheese, cubed
¼ c. onion, chopped
1 c. imitation crabmeat, shredded
½ c. parmesan cheese
4 tsp. lemon juice

Drain and mash artichokes with a fork. Place into a large bowl with remaining ingredients. Stir to blend and pour into a greased crock. Cover and cook on low for 1-2 hours or on high for 30-45 minutes. Serve with crackers (Triskets or Wheat Thins) or corn tortillas (Frito scoops are our favorite!). Great warm or chilled.

Your guest will feel like they are in a fancy restaurant when you serve this.

Be prepared...it won't last long!

So have some before your guests arrive!

Smoking Smokies

2 (16oz.) mini-smoked sausage links
$\frac{3}{4}$ c. hot barbeque sauce
$\frac{1}{4}$ c. Texas Pete hot sauce

Put all ingredients into your crock. Stir to cover sausages with sauce. Cover and cook on low for 4 hours.
(I highly recommend Wild Rooster's Wild Tomato sauce if you really want hot! You can pick up a jar when you go to Cracker Barrel.)

Hot lovers...this one's for you!

The Best Meatballs

1 c. ketchup
$\frac{1}{2}$ c. chili sauce
1 T. soy sauce
1 c. brown sugar
1-2 bags frozen meatballs
(Regular, not Italian)

Pour meatballs into your crock. In a bowl, combine remaining ingredients and pour over meatballs. Cover and cook on low for 3-4 hours.

Delicious and so easy to prepare.
You don't need to thaw
the meatballs before cooking...
making this even quicker!

Cheese Fondue

$\frac{1}{4}$ c. butter
$\frac{1}{4}$ c. flour
$\frac{1}{2}$ tsp. salt
$\frac{1}{4}$ tsp. pepper
$\frac{1}{4}$ tsp. ground mustard
$\frac{1}{4}$ tsp. Worcestershire sauce
1-$\frac{1}{2}$ c. milk
2 c. shredded cheddar cheese

Combine all ingredients in your crock. Cover and cook on low for 2-3 hours. Turn crock off and allow to thicken. Stir well before serving.

This is wonderful with bread cubes, broccoli and ham. It's best to use sharp cheddar cheese for this... gives it a nice bite.

Hot Chocolate

8 c. water
3 c. powdered milk
1/3 c. non-dairy coffee creamer
1 c. Nesquick chocolate milk mix

Pour water into your crock. Add remaining ingredients and stir well. Cover and cook on high for 2-3 hours. Reduce heat to low until ready to serve.

Nothing makes you feel cozier than a warm cup of hot chocolate on a cold day. When serving, top with marshmallows, of course.

Hot Mulled Cider

1 (2 qt.) bottle apple juice
$\frac{1}{2}$ c. honey
1 tsp. allspice
1 tsp. ground cloves
2 cinnamon sticks

Combine all ingredients into your crock. Cook on high for 1 hour. Turn heat to low and cook for at least 2 hours before serving.

If you really want a "wow" effect, serve with orange slices in each cup. This is the perfect holiday beverage!

Peach Spiced Cider

2 (46 oz.) bottles Peach Juicy-Juice
2 c. apple juice
$\frac{1}{4}$ tsp. ground ginger
$\frac{1}{4}$ tsp. cinnamon
$\frac{1}{4}$ tsp. nutmeg
4 fresh orange slices, $\frac{1}{4}$ inch thick

Combine all ingredients into your crock. Top with orange slices. Cover and cook on low for 4-6 hours. Stir before serving.

This warm peach delight absolutely screams "Southern"! It's amazing how a beverage can make an ordinary affair something special.

Tropical Tea

6 regular tea bags or 3 "family size"
6 c. boiling water
1/3 c. sugar
1-½ c. orange juice
2 T. honey
1-½ c. pineapple juice
1 orange sliced with peel on (optional)

Rinse your crock with warm water to prepare it for the boiling water. Place tea bags in and pour boiling water over. Cover and let stand for 5 minutes. Press the tea bags with a spoon before removing them from the crock.Add remaining ingredients. Cover and cook on low for 2-3 hours.

I boil my water in the microwave and pour it into my warm crock straight out of the dishwasher. Decaffeinated tea bags work just fine in this recipe. This is a very good drink served chilled, too.

Meals in Bowls

Soups, Stews & Chilies

Famous Black Bean Soup

¾ c. onions, diced
¾ c. celery, diced
½ c. carrots, diced
¼ c. green pepper, diced
2 T. minced garlic
2 T. vegetable oil
4 (15oz.) cans black beans, drained
2 (14oz.) cans chicken broth
½ tsp. cumin
½ tsp. salt
2 T. cider vinegar
½ tsp. Cayenne pepper
¼ tsp. liquid smoke
2 tsp. chili powder

In a saucepan, cook onion, celery, carrot, green pepper and garlic in oil until tender. In a food processor, process 2 cans of the beans until smooth.Combine all ingredients into your crock including remaining whole beans. Cover and cook on low for 4-6 hours or high for 2-3 hours.

This is one of my most requested recipes and I do believe you will love it! Serve with tortilla chips, a batch of cornbread or a grilled cheese sandwich for the perfect meal!

Taco Soup

1 lb. ground beef
1 onion, chopped
1 (16oz.) can chili beans
1 (15oz.) can kidney beans
1 (15oz.) can whole corn
1 (8oz.) tomato sauce or ketchup
2 c. water
2 (15oz.) cans diced tomatoes
1 (4oz.) can chopped green chilies
1 envelope taco seasoning mix

In a skillet, brown the ground beef and onion. Drain and put into your crock. Add remaining ingredients. (Do not drain any of the canned vegetables.) Stir to blend. Cover and cook on low for 8 hours.

Perfect on a cool night with grilled cheese sandwiches. Top with a dollop of sour cream and/or crushed Fritos. For a little more kick, instead of two cans of diced tomatoes, replace one can with a (16 oz.) jar of salsa.

Easy Vegetable Soup

1 (29oz.) can spaghetti sauce
4 c. water
1 (16oz.) frozen mixed vegetables
1 (8oz.) cooked pasta, optional

Combine sauce and water into your crock. Add vegetables and stir to mix. Cover and cook on low for 6-8 hours. Add pasta during last hour of cooking.

This is surprisingly tasty to be such a simple recipe. Serve with bread or garlic toast for a quick meal.

Potato Soup

8 c. chopped, peeled potatoes
1 onion, chopped
½ lb. bacon, cooked and crumbled
1 (8oz.) cream cheese, softened
3 (14oz.) cans chicken broth
1 can cream of chicken soup
¼ tsp. pepper

Place potatoes, onion and bacon into your crock. In a bowl, combine remaining ingredients. Pour over potatoes and stir to cover. Cover and cook on low for 8-10 hours or high for about 5 hours.

If desired, mash some of the potatoes to thicken the soup.

Cheesy Potato Soup

1 (32oz.) bag frozen southern-style
hash brown potatoes, thawed
½ c. onion, chopped
2 (14oz.) cans chicken broth
1 c. water
3 T. flour
1 c. milk
1 (8oz.) bag shredded cheddar cheese
4-6 slices bacon, cooked and crumbled

Combine potatoes, onion, broth and water in your crock. Cover and cook on low for 6-8 hours. Measure milk into a measuring cup and add flour. Stir to mix. Add to crock and stir. Increase heat to high. Cover and cook for 20-30 minutes or until thickened. Add cheese and stir until melted. When serving, garnish each bowl of soup with bacon crumbles.

Using frozen hash browns
makes this soup go together quickly.
It's so nice not to have to peel and
dice the potatoes.

Corn Chowder

2-½ c. milk
1 can cream style corn
1 can cream of mushroom soup
1 can whole corn
2 medium potatoes, peeled & diced
1 c. cooked ham
1 onion, chopped
2 T. butter
salt and pepper to taste

Combine all ingredients in your crock.
Cover and cook on low for 6-8 hours.

It just doesn't get any easier than this! To make this soup even quicker, replace the potatoes with 1 cup of frozen shredded hash browns.

Beef Stew

1 lb. stewing beef
1 onion, diced
salt and pepper
1 T. vegetable oil
3-4 potatoes, peeled & cubed
1-2 sweet potatoes, peeled & cubed
1 (8oz.) bag baby carrots
3-4 stalks celery,cut into 1 inch pieces
1 can green beans
1 can cream of mushroom soup
1 can peas
1 can whole corn
1 can tomato soup

Brown the beef and onion in a skillet with the oil. Salt and pepper to taste. Place into your crock and add remaining ingredients. (Do not drain canned vegetables.) Stir well. Cover and cook on low for 8-9 hours or on high for 4-5 hours.

This is a hearty meal in a bowl! This is one of the very best stews I have ever had.
If there are leftovers,
this stew freezes well.

Crockin' Chili

2 lbs. ground beef
1 lb. sausage
1 onion, chopped
1 (15oz) dark kidney beans, drained
2 (15oz.) light kidney beans, drained
1 (28oz.) diced tomatoes, do not drain
1 (12oz.) tomato paste
1 T. chili powder
2 tsp. black pepper
hot sauce to taste

In a skillet, brown ground beef and sausage. Drain and pour into your crock. Add remaining ingredients. Cover and cook on low for 4-5 hours.

This is one of our favorite chili recipes.
It is great for warming up
a cold weather dinner.

Corny Chili

1 lb. ground beef
1 onion, chopped
1 (16oz.) kidney beans, drained
2 (14oz.) diced tomatoes, do not drain
1 (14oz.) whole corn, drained
$\frac{3}{4}$ c. salsa, as hot as you like
1 T. chili powder
$\frac{1}{4}$ tsp. garlic powder
pepper to taste

In a skillet, brown ground beef and onion. Drain and pour into your crock. Add remaining ingredients and stir well. Cover and cook on low for 6-8 hours or on high for 4-5 hours.

When serving, we like to top each bowl of chili with shredded cheese, sour cream or corn chips.

Mexicali Chicken Soup

1 (15oz.) Mexican corn, drained
2 (15oz.) chicken broth
1 (10oz.) can chunk chicken
1 (15oz.) black beans
1 (10oz.) diced tomatoes with green
chili peppers, drained

Combine all ingredients in your crock. Stir well. Cover and cook on low for 4-6 hours.

No one will believe that this recipe came from opening 6 cans! Instead of eating like a soup, this can be served over tortilla chips and topped with cheese. If you don't have canned chicken, 1 cup of cooked chicken can replace the can.

Buffalo Chicken Soup

6 c. milk
3 cans cream of chicken soup
3 c. cooked, shredded chicken
1 c. sour cream
¾ to 1 c. Texas Pete hot sauce
½ tsp. pepper

Combine all ingredients in your crock.
Cover and cook on low for 4-5 hours.

If you like hot wings, then this soup's for you. Serve with a cool, green salad to help cut the hot. To make this even easier, use canned, cooked chicken for a quick meal.

Clam Chowder

4 (6 ½oz.)cans minced clams with juice
½ lb. bacon, cut into small pieces
½ c. onion, chopped
6-8 medium potatoes, peeled & diced
3 c. water
1 T. salt
¼ tsp. pepper
4 c. milk
2-2/3c. instant potato flakes

In a skillet, cook bacon and onion. Drain. In your crock, combine clams with juice, bacon, onion, potatoes, water, salt and pepper. Cover and cook on high for 3-4 hours or until potatoes are tender. Add milk and potato flakes. Stir well. Cover and cook for 10-20 minutes or until heated through and thickened.

Yum! This makes a crock full. If you don't need so much, you can easily halve this recipe.

Supreme Seafood Chowder

1 can cream of potato soup
1 can cream of mushroom soup
2-1/2 c. milk
4 carrots, finely chopped
2 potatoes, peeled & diced
1 onion, finely chopped
2 stalks celery, finely chopped
1 (6 oz.) can chopped clams, drained
1 (4 oz.) can tiny shrimp, drained
1 (6 oz.) can crabmeat, drained

In your crock, combine soups and milk. Stir in vegetables. Cover and cook on low for 4-5 hours. Stir in clams, shrimp and crab. Cover and heat 20-30 minutes.

This is a fabulous soup that goes together so easily you might feel a little guilty when all the praise starts coming in. Just smile and enjoy!

Veggies & Side Dishes

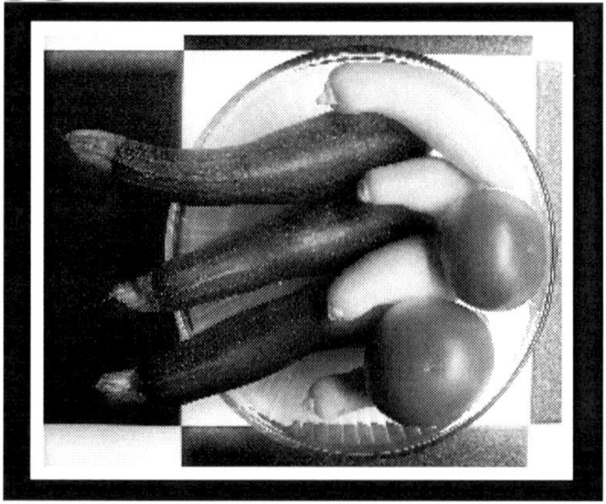

Spinach Casserole

2 (10oz.) frozen chopped spinach
2 c. small-curd cottage cheese
1 c. shredded cheddar cheese
1 egg
2 T. butter, cubed
$\frac{1}{4}$ c. flour
$\frac{1}{2}$ tsp. salt
1 c. Durkee's fried onions, optional

Thaw spinach and squeeze excess liquid out. Combine all ingredients and ½ cup of the fried onions in your crock. Cover and cook on low for 3-4 hours. Top with remaining onions before serving.

This is perfect to serve with steak or pork. It's nice to be able to prepare it, leave it alone and know it will be ready when the main dish is done.

Creamy Corn

1 (16oz.) bag frozen whole kernel corn
1 (8oz.) pkg. cream cheese
1 stick of butter
½ c. milk
1 T. sugar
salt and pepper to taste

Combine all ingredients in your crock. Stir to mix. Cover and cook on low for 4-6 hours.

O.K. now, I won't say this is for the calorie counters out there, but it is very good. This is great for special occasion meals when you are busy with the main dish right up to serving time.

Baked Beans

1 lb. ground beef
4 (16oz.) baked beans with pork,
drain 2 of the cans of beans
1 (4oz.) green chili peppers
1 small onion, chopped (optional)
1 c. barbeque sauce
½ c. brown sugar
1 tsp. garlic powder
1 T. chili powder
1 T. hot pepper sauce

In a skillet, brown the ground beef. Drain and transfer to your crock. Add remaining ingredients. Cover and cook on low for 4-5 hours or on high for 2 hours.

These beans are a nice side dish for BBQ, hot dogs and hamburgers or as a meal with a batch of cornbread.

Cheesy Potatoes

2 cans cheddar cheese soup
1-1/3 c. milk
2 T. butter, melted
½ tsp. seasoned salt
¼ tsp. garlic powder
¼ tsp. pepper
1 (32oz.) frozen cubed hash browns
¼ c. Parmesan cheese
1 tsp. paprika

In your crock, combine soup, milk, butter, seasoned salt, garlic powder and pepper. Mix well. Add potatoes and stir to cover. Top with Parmesan cheese and paprika. Cover and cook on low for 4-5 hours or until potatoes are tender.

Using frozen hash browns makes this recipe go together in no time. Short on time and don't want to peel potatoes? Try this one.

Mashed Potatoes

2 $\frac{1}{2}$ lbs. potatoes, peeled & diced
$\frac{1}{4}$ c. water
1 stick butter, melted
1 tsp. salt
$\frac{1}{4}$ tsp. pepper
$\frac{3}{4}$ c. milk, or more if needed

Combine all ingredients, except milk, in your crock. Stir well. Cover and cook on low for 6-8 hours or on high for 4-5 hours. Using a hand mixer, mash potatoes while still in crock. Add milk to desired consistency. Keep warm on low until ready to serve.

We love mashed potatoes, but it's so hard
to have them ready and warm
at the right time.
This recipe solves everything!

"Baked" Potatoes in the Crock

4-6 medium baking potatoes <u>or</u>
sweet potatoes

butter

Prick the potatoes several times with a fork. Rub each with butter and place into your crock. Cover and cook on low for 6-10 hours or on high for 3-5 hours.

You won't mind getting your hands a little messy...this is so much more convenient than baking potatoes for an hour in the oven.

Classic Sweet Potatoes

¼ c. maple syrup
¼ c. apple juice
1 T. butter
4 small sweet potatoes,
    peeled & quartered
½ c. raisins, optional

In your crock, stir together syrup and juice. Add butter, potatoes and raisins. Cover and cook on low for 4-6 hours.

When sweet potatoes are coming in, I'm always looking for different ways to prepare them. This is one of my favorites and I think you will agree.
It's great to be able to enjoy the season!

Corn Stuffing Balls

½ c. celery, chopped (optional)
¼ c. onion, chopped
1 (14oz.) can cream-style corn
¼ c. water
1/8 tsp. pepper
1 tsp. poultry seasoning
1 (8oz.)box herb flavored stuffing mix
2 eggs, slightly beaten
¼ c. butter, melted

In a bowl, combine all ingredients except butter. Allow to set for 5-10 minutes. Shape stuffing into 7-8 balls. Place into a greased crock and pour butter over all. Cover and cook on low for 3-4 hours.

The mixture will seem a little loose, but the stuffing will be firm after cooking. This is fantastic dressing that makes any day feel like a holiday!

Squash Stuffing Casserole

$\frac{1}{4}$ c. flour
1 can cream of chicken soup
1 c. sour cream
2 medium yellow squash
2 medium zucchini
1 small onion, chopped
1 c. shredded carrots
1 (8oz.)box herb flavored stuffing mix
$\frac{1}{4}$ c. butter, melted

In a bowl, combine the flour, soup and sour cream. Cut squash and zucchini into ½ inch slices. Add vegetables to soup mixture and stir to coat. In another bowl, combine stuffing mix and butter. Pour half of the stuffing mixture into your crock and top with vegetable mixture. Top with remaining half of stuffing mixture. Cover and cook on low for 4-5 hours or until vegetables are tender.

For those who don't care for zucchini, use 4 medium yellow squash instead of the zucchini.

Tomato and Rice Casserole

2 T. butter, melted
2 c. cooked rice
1 (15oz.) diced tomatoes, do not drain
<u>OR</u> 4 -5 tomatoes, peeled & chopped
$\frac{1}{4}$ c. onion, chopped
$\frac{1}{2}$ tsp. salt
$\frac{1}{4}$ tsp. pepper
4 T. Parmesan cheese, optional

Combine all ingredients in your crock except cheese. Stir well. Cover and cook on low for 3-4 hours. Sprinkle with cheese before serving.

You can add 1 cup of sliced okra (fresh or frozen) for a gumbo-like side dish. Mexican or Italian diced tomatoes can be used for a change of flavor. This is a great way to use leftover rice.

Chili Pepper Grits

2 c. quick-cooking grits
6 c. water
½ tsp. cayenne pepper
1 tsp. salt
1 (8oz.)shredded Mexican cheese
1 (4oz.) can green chili peppers
1 or more jalapeno peppers,
seeded & chopped (optional)

Combine all ingredients in your crock and stir well. Cover and cook on low for 6-9 hours or on high for 2-3 hours or until grits are done and thickened. Stir occasionally. If grits become too thick while cooking, add a little water.

We like to serve this warm as a side dish or for brunch with bacon. It can be also be chilled in a loaf pan, sliced and fried in butter like polenta.

Beef

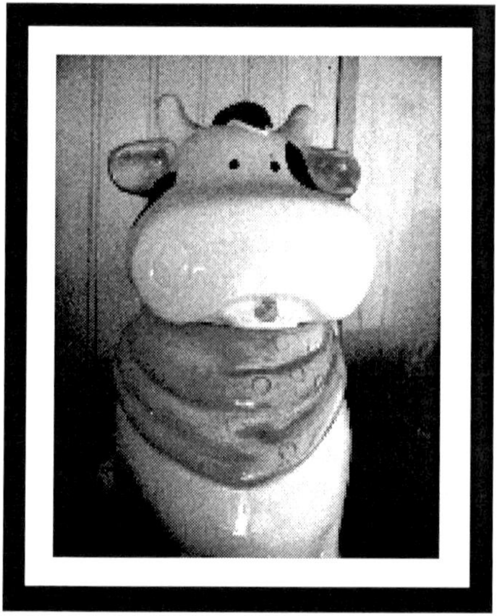

Meaty Spaghetti Sauce

1 (26 oz.) jar spaghetti sauce
1-$\frac{1}{2}$ c. water
1 lb. lean ground beef
$\frac{1}{4}$ c. onion, finely chopped
$\frac{1}{2}$ c. ketchup
1 quick-cooking oats

Combine sauce and water in your crock. In a bowl, combine remaining ingredients and form into 1 inch balls. Place meatballs into sauce. Gently stir to cover meatballs with sauce. Cover and cook on low for 6 hours. Serve over noodles.

I love that you don't have to cook the meat before adding it to the crock. Forming the meat into balls allows it to cook properly. Most of the meatballs will come apart...
that's OK-it thickens the sauce!

Complete Spaghetti

1 lb. frozen precooked meatballs <u>OR</u>
1 lb. ground beef, browned
1 (26oz.) jar spaghetti sauce
1 onion, chopped (optional)
2 c. water
1 (8oz.) pkg. spaghetti noodles

Combine frozen meatballs or cooked ground beef, sauce, onion, and water in your crock. Cover and cook on low for 6-8 hours. Break noodles into 3 inch pieces and stir into sauce. Cover and cook on high for 1 hour. Stir several times while the noodles are cooking.

Do you believe how easy this is?
And the best part?
No boiling noodles!

Crockin' Ravioli

1 jar spaghetti sauce
1 (25oz.) bag frozen beef
  or cheese ravioli
1 (8oz.) can tomato sauce
1-½ c. water
½ tsp. Italian seasoning
1 c. shredded mozzarella

Pour half of the spaghetti sauce into your crock. Add ravioli. In a bowl, combine remaining sauce, tomato sauce and water. Pour over ravioli. Sprinkle Italian seasoning, then cheese over top. Cover and cook on low for 5-7 hours or until ravioli is tender.

OK y'all, it just doesn't get any easier than this. If your sauce starts to get too thick, add another ½ c. of water.

Crockin' Meatloaf

2 lbs. lean ground beef

2 eggs

3 slices of bread, cut into cubes

½ c. milk

2 tsp. salt

1/8 tsp. pepper

½ small onion, chopped

Combine all ingredients and form into a loaf. Place into your crock. Combine sauce ingredients and pour sauce over top. Cover and cook on low for 6-8 hours.

Sauce:

½ c. ketchup

6 T. brown sugar

3 T. mustard

This meatloaf slices nicely and if you have leftovers, makes a great sandwich!

Incredible Spaghetti Sauce

1-½ lb. ground beef
2 onions, chopped
1 tsp. minced garlic
1/3 c. Zesty Italian dressing
½ c. brown sugar
1 c. ketchup
1 c. water
3 cans diced tomatoes, not drained
1 T. Italian seasoning
1 T. salt
1 tsp. pepper
1-2 T.cornstarch

In a skillet, brown the ground beef, onion and garlic. Drain. Pour into a your crock and add remaining ingredients except cornstarch. Cover and cook on low for 6-8 hours. Add cornstarch. Cook, uncovered until thickened.

I have been making the same spaghetti sauce for years until I tried this sauce....now we have two favorite sauces. The Zesty Italian dressing adds a fabulous flavor.

Pizza in a Pot

1 (12oz.) bag wide egg noodles, cooked
1-½ lb. ground beef
¼ c. onion, chopped
1 jar spaghetti sauce
1 (4oz.) sliced mushrooms, drained
1-½ tsp. Italian seasoning
1 (3-½ oz.) pkg. sliced pepperoni
3 c. shredded mozzarella cheese
3 c. shredded cheddar cheese

In a skillet, brown ground beef and onion. Drain and add spaghetti sauce, mushrooms and Italian seasoning. Spread 1/3 of the sauce into a greased crock. Cover with 1/3 of the noodles and pepperoni. Sprinkle with 1/3 of cheeses and repeat layers twice. Cover and cook on low for 3-4 hours.

Super cheesy...
kids and husbands love this one!

Tamale Pie

¾ c. cornmeal
1-½ c. milk
1 c. shredded cheddar cheese
1 egg
1 lb. ground beef
1 envelope chili seasoning mix
1 (16oz.) diced tomatoes, do not drain
¼ c. onion, diced
1 tsp. seasoning salt
1 (16oz.) can whole corn, drained
1 (2-¼ oz.) black olives

In a skillet, brown ground beef and drain. In a large bowl, combine cornmeal, milk and egg. Add ground beef and remaining ingredients except for the cheese. Pour into your crock. Cover and cook on high for 3-4 hours. Sprinkle with cheese and cook for 10 more minutes or until cheese is melted.

This is like a thick chili. Delicious served in a bowl and topped with sour cream.

Crockin' Enchiladas

1 lb. ground beef
1 env. taco seasoning mix (low salt)
1-$\frac{1}{4}$ c. water
1 (16oz.) jar chunky salsa
1 can cream of chicken soup
1 can cream of mushroom soup
3 c. Mexican blend shredded cheese
10 (6 inch) corn or flour tortillas

In a skillet, brown ground beef and drain. Add taco seasoning mix and water. Simmer for 15 minutes. In a bowl, stir together salsa, and soups. Add 2 cups of the cheese and mix well. Cut tortillas into quarters. Place a layer of tortillas into the bottom of your crock. Layer with 1/3 of the meat then with 1/3 of the cheese. Repeat layers twice. The top layer will be tortillas. Sprinkle with 1 cup of cheese. Cover and cook on low for 3-4 hours or on high for 45 minutes to 1 hour.

Beef Tips

2 lbs. stew beef

1 onion, chopped

3 T. vegetable oil

2 c. water

1 env. brown gravy mix

¼ c. soy sauce

¼ c. Worcestershire sauce

½ tsp. garlic powder

½ tsp. pepper

1 (4oz.) can sliced mushrooms, drained

Pound meat with a meat mallet and cut into bite size pieces. In a skillet, sauté onion in oil until tender. Add the meat and brown on all sides. (This only take 3-5 minutes. Don't over cook it.) In your crock combine water, gravy mix, soy sauce, Worcestershire sauce, garlic powder, pepper and mushrooms. Add browned meat and onions. Cover and cook on low for 5-7 hours. If you want a thicker sauce, uncover for the last hour of cooking. Serve over rice.

A real family pleaser!

Steak Rolls

1 (4oz.) can sliced mushrooms, drained

2 T. butter, melted

1 (6oz.) box herb flavored stuffing mix

1 (1-$\frac{3}{4}$ lb.) flank steak

1 envelope brown gravy mix

$\frac{1}{4}$ c. onion, chopped

1 c. water

1 beef bouillon cube

2 T. flour

2 T. water

In a bowl, stir together mushrooms, butter and stuffing mix. Spread over center of steak. Roll steak from the long end. Tie with kitchen string or hold together with toothpicks. Place into your crock. Prepare gravy mix according to directions and pour over meat. Add onions. Dissolve bouillon cube in water in microwave and add to meat. Cover and cook on low for 8-10 hours. To thicken the juices, remove meat from pot. Combine flour and 2 T. water. Cover and cook on high for 20-30 minutes.

Steak Burritos

2 lbs. flank or round steak
1 envelopes taco seasoning
1 large onion, chopped
½ c. sliced jalapenos from a jar
1 T. vinegar
10 (7 inch) flour tortillas

Toppings:

shredded Monterey Jack cheese
salsa
sour cream

Rub both sides of steaks with taco seasoning. Place into greased crock. Add onion, jalapenos and vinegar. Cover and cook on low for 8-9 hours. Remove from pot and shred with a knife and fork. Return meat to pot and cook until heated through. Using a slotted spoon, place about ½ cup of meat onto the center of tortilla. Top with cheese, salsa and sour cream, as desired.

One (4 oz.) can of green chilies can replace the jalapenos if you don't want as much kick.

Beef & Broccoli

1 ($\frac{3}{4}$-1 lb.) round steak
1 envelope brown gravy mix
1/2 c. water
$\frac{3}{4}$ c. soy sauce
1 tsp. crushed red pepper
$\frac{1}{2}$ tsp. minced garlic
1 bunch fresh broccoli

Cut steak across the grain into thin strips and place into your crock. In a bowl, mix gravy mix, water, soy sauce, red pepper and garlic. Stir well and pour into crock. Cover and cook on low for 4-6 hours. Cut broccoli into flowerets and add to crock. Cover and cook for another 1-2 hours. Serve over rice.

The meat is much easier to cut if it is semi-frozen. If you want a little more zing, add more crushed red pepper. Don't use frozen broccoli - it gets way too mushy.

Mushroom Beef

1-$\frac{1}{2}$ lb. bottom round steak
1 can beef gravy
1 T. Worcestershire sauce
1 T. Dijon mustard
2 (4oz.) sliced mushrooms, drained

Cut beef into thin slices. Place all ingredients in your crock. Cover and cook on low for 6-8 hours. Serve over noodles, rice or mashed potatoes.

If you want to thicken the gravy, combine 2 T. flour with 2 T. water. Stir well and add to crock. Cook for 20-30 minutes more or until thickened.

Steak Teriyaki

2 lbs. round steak
1 T. sugar
½ c. soy sauce
1 tsp. ground ginger
2 T. vegetable oil
1 tsp. minced garlic
1 (16oz.) bag frozen stir-fry
vegetables, thawed

Cut steak into bite size pieces. Place into your crock. In a bowl, combine ingredients except vegetables. Pour over meat. Add vegetables. Stir well. Cover and cook on low for 6-8 hours.Serve over rice. *I love that you don't have to cook the meat before putting it in the crock. This is a perfect meal to prepare on days when you are on the run between games, practices and meetings. We all have days when we think there is no time to prepare a meal. This can be put together the night before and turned on in the morning.*

No-Fry Steak and Gravy

1-2 lbs. cube steak
1 can cream of mushroom soup
1 T. onion, minced
1 soup can of water
1 (4oz.) sliced mushrooms, drained
pepper to taste

Cut steaks into bite size pieces and place into your crock. In a bowl, combine remaining ingredients and pour over steak. Cover and cook on low for 10-12 hours. Serve over rice.

I love that you don't have to brown the steaks before adding to the crock. This is a great time saving recipe!

Barbeque Beef

1 (2-½ lb.) chuck roast

Rub:

1 tsp. salt
1 tsp. chili powder
½ tsp. garlic powder
¼ tsp. onion salt
¼ tsp. pepper

Sauce:

2 T. cider vinegar
½ c. ketchup
½ c. chili sauce
¼ c. brown sugar
1 tsp. liquid smoke
½ tsp. ground mustard
2 T. Worcestershire sauce

In a small bowl, combine rub ingredients. Rub spices over all sides of roast and place into your crock. Make sauce and pour half over roast. Cover and cook on high for 4-5 hours. Serve with remaining half of sauce. Serve on buns.

Incredible!
You have to try this...we have a hard time not eating it all before it gets put on a bun!

Roast with Potatoes

1 onion, sliced
1 (3 lb.) bottom round beef roast
3 baking potatoes, cubed
1 c. baby carrots
1 tsp. minced garlic
1 can beef broth, divided
1 envelope onion soup mix
¼ c. flour

Put sliced onion in your crock. Top with roast and place potatoes and garlic around sides. In a bowl, mix 1-¼ cup of broth with soup mix. Pour over roast. Cover and cook on low for 9-10 hours. Remove meat and vegetables from crock. Combine remaining ½ cup of broth with flour. Gradually stir into juices in pot. Cover and increase heat to high. Cook for 15 minutes or until thickened. Serve over rice with meat and vegetables.

Fabulous Roast

1 (2-$\frac{1}{2}$ to 3-$\frac{1}{2}$ lb.) beef roast
1 envelope brown gravy mix
1 envelope Italian dressing mix
1 envelope Ranch dressing mix
$\frac{1}{2}$ c. water

In your crock, combine dry mixes. Add roast and cover all sides of roast with mixture. Add water around the roast. Cover and cook on low for 6-8 hours. If you use a meat thermometer, when it reads 170* it's done. To make gravy, remove meat from the crock. In a measuring cup, combine ¼ cup water with ¼ cup cornstarch. Stir into liquid in pot. Turn heat to high and cook for 15-30 minutes. *Make rice while your gravy is cooking and you'll have a fantastic dinner with very little effort.*

Pork

& Seafood

Crockin' Ham

1 (5 lb.) canned ham
½ c. brown sugar
1 tsp. dry mustard
1 tsp. prepared horseradish
¼ c. cola, not diet

Place ham into your crock. In a small bowl or measuring cup, combine the brown sugar, dry mustard, horseradish and 1 T. of the cola. Spread over ham and pour remaining cola around the ham in the crock. Cover and cook on low for 8-10 hours.

My grandmother taught me the secret of cooking ham in cola. She cooks hers on the stove, but it's so much easier in the crock. You don't have to keep an eye on it.

Pork Barbeque

1 (3-4 lbs.) boneless pork roast
1-½ tsp. seasoned salt
1 tsp. garlic powder
1 c. barbeque sauce
1 c. cola (not diet)

Sprinkle roast with seasoned salt and garlic powder. Cover and cook on low for 4 hours. Remove meat from crock and pour out liquid. Shred the meat with a knife and fork and return to crock. Combine the barbeque sauce and cola. Pour over the meat. Cover and cook on high for 1-2 hours. Serve on buns.

I always hear lots of "yums" when I serve this fantastic barbeque. The cola and barbeque sauce cook into a nice thick sauce for the pork that you and you family will love!

Tender Pork Roast

1 (3 lb.) boneless, pork roast
1 (8 oz.) tomato sauce
¾ c. soy sauce
½ c. sugar
2 tsp. ground mustard

Place roast into your crock. In a small bowl or measuring cup, combine remaining ingredients and pour over roast. Cover and cook on low for 8-9 hours. Remove meat from crock and shred or chop it. Add some of the sauce from the crock to the shredded meat. Serve on buns.

The perfect busy day meal. Pick up some buns on the way home and dinner is ready!

Barbeque Ribs

4-5 lbs. boneless pork spareribs
1 onion, sliced
1 c. ketchup
½ c. water
¼ c. brown sugar
¼ c. cider vinegar
2 T. Worcestershire sauce
2 tsp. ground mustard
1-½ tsp. salt
1 tsp. paprika

Cut ribs into serving size pieces and place half of them into your crock. Top with half of the onion slices and repeat layers. In a bowl, combine remaining ingredients and pour over all. Cover and cook on low for 8-9 hours.

I like this recipe because you don't have to brown or boil the ribs before cooking them with the sauce. Easy!

Smoky Apple Butter Ribs

3 lb. boneless, country-style ribs
¼ tsp. salt
½ tsp. pepper
1 onion, sliced
½ c. apple butter
2 T. brown sugar
1 T. liquid smoke
1 tsp. minced garlic

Cut ribs into serving size pieces and place into your crock. Salt and pepper ribs, then layer with onion slices. In a bowl, combine remaining ingredients and pour over ribs. Cover and cook on low for 6-8 hours.

Apple butter lovers I doubt you've ever had it like this before. The apple butter adds a wonderful flavor to these ribs.

Chicken Fried Chops

$\frac{1}{2}$ c. flour
2 tsp. salt
1-$\frac{1}{2}$ tsp. ground mustard
$\frac{1}{2}$ tsp. garlic powder
6 thick pork chops
2 T. vegetable oil
1 can cream of chicken soup
1/3 c. water

In a shallow bowl, combine flour, salt, mustard and garlic powder. Dredge the chops in this mixture. In a skillet, brown both sides of chops and place into your crock. In a bowl, combine soup and water and pour over chops. Cover and cook on low for 6-8 hours. To thicken the juices, remove meat and add 2 T. flour mixed into 2 T. water. Cover and cook on high for 20-30 minutes. *It may seem like extra work to brown the chops before cooking them, but you won't mind when you taste these. Definitely worth the effort.*

Fancy Ham Slices

1/3 c. pecans, chopped (optional)
2 (½ inch thick) ham slices
1 c. maple syrup
½ c. water
3 T. sugar
2 T. butter, melted

Toast pecans by placing them into a shallow pan and baking at 325* for 5-10 minutes or until they are lightly browned. Set aside. In your crock, combine the maple syrup, water, sugar and butter. Stir well. In a skillet, brown the ham slices on each side and add to your crock. Cover and cook on low for 2-4 hours. Before serving, top with toasted pecans.

I like to buy the ham slices when they are on sale and I'm always looking for a new way to prepare them...this is a good alternative to just pan frying them.

Kielbasa with Cabbage

1 lb. Kielbasa or smoked sausage,
  cut into 1 inch pieces
1 small head of cabbage
2 potatoes, diced
1 tsp. salt
pepper to taste
1 onion, thinly sliced
1 (14oz.) can chicken broth

In your crock, layer half of all ingredients except chicken broth. Repeat layers and pour broth over all. Cover and cook on low for 6-8 hours or high for 3-4 hours.

Your crock will be very full when you start cooking, don't worry...keep a lid on it and it will go down as it cooks.
We like this just as it is, but it can be served over rice.

Cheesy Potatoes and Kielbasa

1 lb. kielbasa or smoked sausage
1 (28 oz.) frozen O'Brien hash browns
with onions & peppers
1 can cream of chicken soup
1 c. shredded cheddar cheese
½ c. water

Cut sausage into 1 inch slices and place into your crock. Add remaining ingredients and stir well. Cover and cook on low for 6-8 hours or until the potatoes are tender.

This is my kind of recipe...dump, slice, stir, cook, and eat. Love it!

Pizza Spaghetti Casserole

1 lb. sausage
1 onion, chopped
1 lb. spaghetti noodles, uncooked
1 (28oz.) jar spaghetti sauce
1 (15oz.) can tomato sauce
¾ c. water
1 (4oz.) sliced mushrooms, drained
1 (6oz.) pkg. pepperoni slices, optional
1 (16oz.) shredded mozzarella cheese

In a skillet, brown sausage and onion. Drain. In a bowl, combine spaghetti sauce, tomato sauce, water and mushrooms. Place 1/3 of sausage and 1/3 of pepperoni into your crock. Top with 1/3 of sauce. Top with 1/3 of spaghetti noodles (broken in half). Repeat layers twice. Top with cheese. Cover and cook on low for 6-8 hours.*I love that you don't have to boil the noodles for this recipe. This is a summer time favorite for us...get it cooking, go out and play, come in and eat! My kind of recipe!*

Sweet & Sour Shrimp

1 (6oz.) frozen sugar pea pods
1 (20oz.) pineapple chunks, save juice
2 T. cornstarch
3 T. sugar
1 cube chicken bouillon
1 c. water
2 tsp. soy sauce
½ tsp. ground ginger
1 lb. shrimp, cooked and peeled
cashews, optional (but recommended)

Place pea pods and drained pineapple in crock. In a small saucepan, stir together ½ cup of the reserved juice and remaining ingredients except shrimp. Bring to a boil. Cook and stir for 1 minute or until slightly thickened. Pour sauce into your crock and gently stir. Cover and cook on low for 4-6 hours. Add shrimp. Cover and cook for 15-20 minutes. Serve over rice and sprinkle with cashews.

To make this even easier, replace shrimp with 2 (4oz.) cans of shrimp, drained.

Soooooooo Good!

Shrimp Marinara

1 green pepper, chopped
½ c. onion, chopped
1 tsp. minced garlic
2 T. vegetable oil
salt and pepper to taste
2 (15oz.) jars salsa (we like medium)
½ c. water
1 lb. shrimp, cooked and peeled

In a skillet, sauté green pepper, onion and garlic in oil until tender. Salt and pepper to taste. Pour into your crock. Add salsa and water. Cover and cook on low for 3-4 hours. Stir in shrimp and cook for 20 minutes more. Serve over rice or spaghetti noodles.

This is so good and easy. Control the flavor with the hotness of the salsa. If you like spicy but not scorching, try using one each of "Hot" and "Medium".

Chicken, Turkey & Eggs

Chicken 'n Dumplin's

3-5 boneless chicken breast halves
2 T. butter, melted
2 cans cream of chicken soup
2 soup cans of water
¼ tsp. pepper
1 (12oz.) can refrigerated biscuits

Place chicken into your crock. In a bowl, combine butter, soups, water and pepper. Pour over chicken. Cover and cook on low for 6-8 hours. An hour before serving, tear chicken with a fork into bite size pieces and add back to crock. Cut biscuits into $\frac{1}{4}$'s and add to crock. Cover and cook on high for 40-45 minutes or until biscuits are done in the center. Gently stir to cover dumplings with sauce.

One of our favorites!

Your chicken can be frozen when you put it into the crock. (Mine usually is...)

Frozen Chicken Pie

3-6 frozen boneless chicken breast
2 cans cream of chicken soup
1 (4oz.) sliced mushrooms, drained
2 (16oz.) cans Veg-All, drained
¼ tsp. salt
¼ tsp. pepper

Place frozen chicken breasts into your crock. In a bowl, combine remaining ingredients and pour over chicken. Cover and cook on low for 8-10 hours.

This is a variation from a recipe in my first book. If your chicken is not frozen, cook for 6-8 hours on low.
We love this over biscuits.

So Easy Chicken Pie

2 cans cream of chicken soup
1 soup can of water
$\frac{1}{4}$ c. butter, melted
1 (15 oz.) can Veg-All
salt and pepper to taste
4 individual frozen chicken pies

In a bowl, combine soup, water, butter, Veg-All, salt and pepper. Stir well. Pour into a greased crock. Place frozen chicken pies on top. Cover and cook on low for 3-4 hours. Stir occasionally to break up pies.

I created this one myself and I'm pretty proud of it! If you need to prepare it and leave it, heat the pies enough to cut them into pieces and add them to the sauce to cook.

Chicken Noodle Casserole

3-6 boneless chicken breasts
$\frac{1}{4}$ c. butter
1 (16oz.) can Veg-All
2 cans cream of chicken soup
2 pkgs. chicken ramen noodles
1 c. water
pepper to taste

Cut chicken into bite size pieces. Combine all ingredients except noodles in your crock. Add only one of the seasoning packets that came with the noodles. Cover and cook on low for 6 hours. Add noodles and stir to cover noodles with sauce. Cover and cook for 1 hour on high.

This is very chicken pie-ish but quick and easy.
If you are pressed for time, don't cut the chicken breasts.

Smokehouse Chicken

1 whole chicken
$\frac{1}{4}$ c. liquid smoke
salt

Rinse chicken and pat dry or remove skin. Salt liberally on all sides and place into your crock. Pour liquid smoke over chicken. Cover and cook on low for 8-10 hours. Turn chicken several times during cooking. To serve, place chicken on a platter to cut.

Wow! You will love this!
Great flavor with little work.
Removing the skin will allow more of the smokehouse flavor into the chicken, this also makes this a very low-fat dish.

Creamy Bacon Chicken

4-6 boneless chicken breasts
one slice of bacon for each breast
2 cans cream of mushroom soup
1 c. sour cream
½ c. flour

Wrap one slice of bacon around each chicken breast and place into your crock. In a bowl, combine soups, sour cream, and flour. Pour over chicken. Cover and cook on low for 6-8 hours.

Serve over rice with a salad for a simple dinner.

Waikiki Chicken

3-6 boneless chicken breast halves
1 green bell pepper, chopped
1 small onion, chopped
1 (20oz.) pineapple chunks, save juice
1 c. soy sauce
2 c. brown sugar
2 tsp. ground ginger
1 T. minced garlic

Place chicken into your crock. Top with green pepper, onion and ½ cup of the pineapple juice. In a small bowl, combine soy sauce, brown sugar, ginger and garlic. Stir well and pour into crock. Cover and cook on high for 1 hour. Reduce heat to low and cook for 6-8 more hours. Serve over rice.

This is a great change from your ordinary chicken dish. The pineapple adds a wonderful flavor to this fun meal.

Southwestern Chicken

2 (15oz.) cans whole corn, drained
1 (15oz.) can black beans, drained
1 (16oz.) jar chunky salsa, divided
3-6 boneless chicken breast halves
1 c. shredded cheddar cheese

Combine corn, beans and ½ cup of salsa in your crock. Top with chicken. Pour remaining salsa over chicken. Cover and cook on low for 7-8 hours or high for 3-4 hours. Sprinkle with cheese. Cover and cook for 5-10 minutes or until cheese is melted.

This is one fantastic meal! I suggest using a medium salsa and serving with sour cream. Yummy!

Red Pepper Chicken

4 boneless chicken breasts
1 (15oz.) black beans, drained
1 (15oz.) jar roasted red peppers
1 (16oz.) jar salsa (med. or hot)
1 onion, chopped
½ tsp. salt
pepper to taste

Place chicken into your crock. In a bowl, combine remaining ingredients. Pour over chicken. Cover and cook on low for 6-8 hours. Serve over rice.

This is a dish that is very easy to assemble and simply elegant.

Jambalaya

1-½ lbs. boneless chicken breasts
1 lb. smoked sausage
1 (28 oz.) can diced tomatoes
1 green pepper, chopped
1 tsp. cayenne pepper
2 tsp. Cajun Seasoning
1 c. chicken broth
1 c. celery, diced
1 tsp. oregano
1 onion, chopped
2 c. rice, cooked
1 lb. shrimp, cooked

Cut chicken into 1 inch cubes and place into your crock. Cut sausage into 1 inch slices and add to pot. Add remaining ingredients except shrimp and rice. Cover and cook on low for 6-8 hours. About 30 minutes before serving, add shrimp and rice. Heat thoroughly before serving.

This is truly "Cajun Hot". If you don't want it too spicy, use only 1 tsp. of Cajun Seasoning.

Oriental Chicken

3-4 lbs. chicken, cut up
2 T. vegetable oil
1/3 c. soy sauce
2 T. brown sugar
2 T. water
1 tsp. minced garlic
1 tsp. ground ginger

In a skillet, brown chicken in oil on both sides. Place chicken into your crock. In a measuring cup, combine remaining ingredients and pour over chicken. Cover and cook on high for 1 hour. Reduce heat to low and cook for 4-5 hours longer.

I like to remove the skin
from the chicken before cooking.
This allows the flavor to penetrate.

Tender Turkey

2 onions, sliced
4-5 lb. turkey breast or breast half
3-4 T. butter
1 tsp. garlic powder
1 tsp. paprika

Place onion slices into your crock and top with turkey breast. Lift skin and put butter underneath. Sprinkle with garlic powder and paprika. Cover and cook on high for 4-½ hours.

If you can't find a turkey breast small enough to fit in your crock, ask the butcher to cut one in half. Freeze the other half for another meal.

Cranberry Chipotle Turkey

1 (15oz.) whole cranberry sauce
1 c. Lawry's Baja Chipotle marinade
3 lb. frozen turkey breast roast

Combine the cranberry sauce and marinade in your crock. Place frozen turkey breast roast on top. (Discard the gravy packet or use it with something else.) Cover and cook on high for 2 hours. Reduce heat to low and cook for 5-8 more hours. Remove roast and cut string off. Shred turkey and stir into cranberry sauce mixture. Serve on buns or rolls.

I have recently discovered the marinades from Lawry's and I have to tell you...they are fantastic. They make it easy to prepare a great meal!

Eggs Florentine

1 c. shredded cheddar cheese
1 (10oz.) frozen spinach, thawed
2 sliced of bread, cubed without crust
1 (4oz.) can sliced mushrooms, drained
¼ c. onions, diced
6 eggs
1 c. milk
½ c. water
½ tsp. salt
¼ tsp. pepper
½ tsp. paprika

Spray your crock well with non-stick cooking spray. Layer: ½ c. cheese, spinach, bread cubes, mushrooms and onions. In a bowl, whisk together eggs, milk, water, salt and pepper. Pour into crock. Sprinkle with remaining cheese and paprika. Cover and cook on high for 1-½ to 2 hours or until center is set.

Wonderful for breakfast or brunch. Be sure to squeeze the excess water out of the spinach before adding to the crock.

Broccoli Egg Casserole

1 (24oz.) small curd cottage cheese
1 (10oz.) frozen, chopped broccoli
2 c. shredded cheddar cheese
6 eggs, beaten
1/3 c. flour
¼ c. butter, melted
3 T. onion, finely chopped
½ tsp. salt

Thaw and drain broccoli. In a large bowl, combine all ingredients. Pour into greased crock. Cover and cook on high for 1 hour. Stir and reduce heat to low. Cover and cook for 2-½ to 3 hours longer or until eggs are set. Sprinkle with additional cheese, if desired.

This is so good and cheesy! Serve as a side dish or for a special brunch.

Desserts

Triple Chocolate Cake

1 box chocolate cake mix
1 (3oz.) instant chocolate pudding mix
2 c. sour cream
1 c. water
4 eggs, beaten
$\frac{3}{4}$ c. vegetable oil
1-$\frac{1}{2}$ c. chocolate chips

In a bowl, combine all ingredients except chocolate chips. Mix well until smooth. Fold in chips and pour batter into a greased crock. Cover and cook on low for 6-7 hours. Remove cover and allow to set for 20-30 minutes before serving.

You have to try this cake. It is good served warm with ice cream, and is even better refrigerated for a day or two. Absolutely fabulous!

Apple Pie

8 tart apples, peeled & sliced
1-$\frac{1}{4}$ tsp. cinnamon
$\frac{1}{4}$ tsp. allspice
$\frac{1}{4}$ tsp. nutmeg
$\frac{3}{4}$ c. milk
2 T. butter
$\frac{3}{4}$ c. sugar
2 eggs

1-$\frac{1}{2}$ c. Bisquick
1/3 c. brown sugar
3 T. butter

2 tsp. vanilla

In a large bowl, toss apples with cinnamon, allspice and nutmeg. Pour into a greased crock. In a bowl, combine milk, 2 T. butter, sugar, eggs, vanilla and ½ c. Bisquick. Spoon mixture over apples. In the same bowl, combine 1 c. Bisquick and brown sugar. Cut in 3 T. butter until crumbly. Sprinkle over apples. Cover and cook on low for 6-7 hours or until apples are soft.

You know what I'm going to say...
this is so good served
warm with vanilla ice cream!

Bread Pudding

8 slices of bread, cubed
4 eggs
2 c. milk
¼ c. sugar
¼ c. butter, melted
¼ c. raisins
½ tsp. cinnamon

<u>Sauce:</u>
2 T. butter
2 T. flour
1 c. water
¾ c. sugar
1 tsp. vanilla

Place bread cubes into a greased crock. In a bowl, beat eggs and milk. Stir in sugar, butter, raisins and cinnamon. Pour over bread. Cover and cook on high for 1 hour. Reduce heat to low and cook for 3-4 hours or until eggs are set. Before serving, prepare sauce. In a saucepot, melt butter. Stir in flour. Gradually add water, sugar and vanilla. Bring to a boil. Cook and stir for 2 minutes or until thickened. Serve over warm bread pudding. *Delicious!*

Sticky Bananas

1 T. butter, melted
4 bananas, peeled
1 tsp. lemon juice
3 T. brown sugar
$\frac{1}{4}$ tsp. cinnamon (optional)

Pour butter into your crock. Slice the bananas diagonally into ½ inch slices and add to crock. Sprinkle lemon juice, brown sugar, and cinnamon over the bananas. Stir to coat bananas well. Cover and cook on low for 2 hours or on high for 1 hour.

To serve, spoon banana mixture over vanilla ice cream or pound cake (or both). Enjoy!

Crockin' Cobbler

1/3 c. Bisquick
2/3 c. quick-cooking oats
¼ tsp. cinnamon
½ c. sugar
½ c. brown sugar
4 c. fruit (sliced peaches, apples or blueberries)

In a bowl, combine all ingredients in order listed. Pour into a greased crock. Cover and cook on low for 4-6 hours.

This is delicious served warm with a dollop of vanilla ice cream.

Crockin' Candy

2 (16 oz.) dry roasted salted peanuts
1 (12oz.) semi-sweet chocolate chips
1 bar German chocolate
1 (32oz.) white almond bark

Place all ingredients into your crock. Cover and cook on low for 1-$\frac{1}{2}$ to 2 hours. Drop rounded spoonfuls onto wax paper and allow to cool.

You will never make candy the hard way again! To make this even easier, pour the chocolate mixture onto wax paper lined cookie sheets. Allow to cool, then break apart. Try with cashews for a special treat!

This 'n That

"Baked" Bread

1 loaf frozen bread dough
butter

Rub bread dough generously with butter and place into a greased crock. Cover and cook on low for 2 hours or until bread is thawed and beginning to rise. Increase setting to high and cook for 2 - 2 ½ hours or until browned.

You will absolutely love having fresh bread straight out of your cooker. Nobody has to know how easy this is. Enjoy!

How to Warm Your Buns with Your Crock

buns for hamburgers, BBQ or hotdogs

OR

rolls for sandwiches or dinner

OR

to refresh semi-stale bread

Pour 1 cup of water into your crock. Arrange 2-3 rings from canning jars or lids from mayonnaise, etc. jars. (You just need something to keep your buns out of the water.) Wrap your buns in foil and set onto the lids. Cover and cook on low for 1 hour. If your buns need to be sliced, cut them before heating them.

You are gonna love me for this recipe. I created it while writing this book. You will never have cold buns again!

"Roasted" Red Peppers

2 lg. red bell peppers, cut into strips
1-2 onions, thinly sliced
3 T. cider vinegar
2 T. brown sugar
1 T. vegetable oil
1 T. honey
¼ tsp. salt
1/8 tsp. red pepper flakes

Combine all ingredients in your crock. Cover and cook on low for 4 hours. Serve warm or chilled.

You will love these peppers with grilled chicken or pork. They are also a great topping for sandwiches.

Basil Infused Oil

1 c. mild olive oil or vegetable oil
1/3 c. packed, chopped fresh basil

Place the oil and basil in your crock. Cover and cook on high for 1-½ to 2 hours. Allow to cool and strain through cheesecloth. Pour into a glass jar and refrigerate for up to 1 month.

Drizzle over fresh tomatoes or brush on bread and toast. Experiment using different fresh herbs. This is a great way to enjoy your herb garden.

Cajun Boiled Peanuts

1 (24 oz.) bag raw peanuts, in shells
water
1 (4oz.) pkg. crab boil
1 (4oz.) can sliced green chilies,
do not drain
$\frac{1}{4}$ c. hot sauce (We like Texas Pete)

Place peanuts in your crock. Add as much water as will fit in your pot. Add crab boil, chilies and hot sauce. Cover and cook on low overnight. Turn crock off and allow to set for 4-5 hours before serving. The longer it sets, the hotter they will be. When they are as hot as you want, remove them from the liquid.

Perfect for ball game parties!

Granola

3 c. quick-cooking oats

1 c. honey

1 c. shredded coconut

$\frac{1}{4}$ c. vegetable oil

$\frac{1}{2}$ c. sesame or sunflower seeds

dash of cinnamon & nutmeg

$\frac{1}{2}$ c. chopped cashews

$\frac{1}{2}$ c. chopped almonds

$\frac{1}{2}$ c. chopped dates

$\frac{1}{2}$ c. raisins

Combine all ingredients except dates and raisins in your crock. Cover with lid slightly ajar. Cook on low for 2-1/2 to 3 hours, stir occasionally. Fold dates and raisins into the granola. Pour onto a wax paper covered cookie sheet and cover with another sheet of wax paper. Press well. Allow to cool then break apart and store in an air-tight container or Ziplock bag.

To keep the lid ajar, place a wooden or heat resistant spoon into the cooking granola. This makes a wonderful cereal, snack or trail mix.

Index

Holiday Suggestions

Soups, Stews & Chilies

Beef, continued

Pork & Seafood

Chicken, Turkey & Eggs, continued

Desserts

Lisa's first book

"From Our Home to Yours"

is a collection of her family's recipes...

with few ingredients

and easy to follow directions.

You and your family can enjoy Bacon Wrapped Chicken, Cinnamon Apple Sweet Potatoes & Corny Cornbread.

"Gritslickers-Southern Home Cooking
for Today's Cooks"
is Lisa's second book...filled with recipes and tips
to help busy cooks
eat more meals at home.

From Fried Okra
to Easy
Chicken & Dumplings-
Lisa's helpful notes
will make you feel
like you have
a friend in the kitchen
guiding you along!

"Lisa Shively's
Fat Little Blueberry Cookbook" is the first in a series of Lisa's specialty books. This book contains 100 delicious recipes featuring blueberries.

This book will give you a new love of blueberries from Blueberry Milkshakes and Blueberry Banana Bread to Blueberry Salsa Full of new favorites and classic standards.

Lisa Shively's Fat Little Crockin' Cookbook is the second book in Lisa's Fat Little Cookbook series. She shares with you recipes that are perfect for busy families in hopes of giving you more time to spend with the ones you love most.

Lisa has 100 recipes from Chicken Cordon Bleu and Big Dave's Mesquite Beef to Crockin' Candy and Sweetheart's Fudge Fondue. You're gonna love this collection!

To Order:

Contact
Lisa Shively Cookbooks
P.O. Box 2123
Eden, NC 27289

Credit card orders can be made online at
www.fromourhometoyours.net
or call 336-623-7511